Notes from the GARDEN

Written in Hard Times,
Revised in Love,
Composed at the end of a trial from above;
Touched by a Hand both unseen and kind
In the Hope that it may bring
One Soul Peace of Mind.

Greg Wright

Copyright © 2017 by Greg Wright

All rights reserved. This book or any portion thereof may not be reproduced or used in any manner whatsoever without the express written permission of the author except for the use of brief quotations in a book review.

ISBN-13: 978-1546455813

ISBN-10: 1546455817

Contact Greg at gregwright10449@hotmail.com

Table of Contents

ABOUT THE BOOK	7
TO MY FATHER, WHO WALKED INTO HEAVEN	11
TWO FREE SECRETS INSIDE!	12
THE BOOKS OF LIFE	13
ONE MINUTE MEDITATION	14
SIT!	15
SONGBIRDS IN SPRING AT DAYBREAK	16
OLD INFORMATION	17
FREEDOM AND HUMAN RIGHTS	18
IT TAKES AN ETERNITY TO GET TO THIS SECOND	19
EXPERIENCE ONLY, PLEASE!	20
SPEAKING OF SILENCE	21
PUTTING MUSIC TO WORDS	22
PICTURE PERFECT	23
THE BEAUTY OF PERCEPTION	24
COSMIC CHICKEN SOUP	25
ARE WE IMMORTAL OR ETERNAL?	26
FIXING EVERYTHING	27
EVOLUTION SOLUTION	28
THE PERCEPTION OF PEACE	29
BEING HERE NOW	30
PLANTING THE SEED	31
WHICH CAME FIRST, THE CHICKEN OR THE EGGESTENTIAL CONCEPT?	32
TRAIN OF THOUGHT	33
GIFTS AND PRESENCE	34
ACTIVITIES PERFORMED WITHOUT MOVING	35
VOICE LESSONS	36

INSIDE/OUT	37
RETURN TO CENTER	38
ONE LIFE	39
CHOICE DECISIONS	40
DON'T BE AFRAID TO THINK ABOUT WHAT YOU KNOW	41
HUMAN EMOTIONS	42
COMPASSION AS AN ALTERNATIVE	43
CHOICE ENCOUNTER	44
ALTERNATIVES	45
EVOLVING IDEALS	46
CONFLUENCE	47
ANGER'S OBITUARY	48
TIME CHANGES	49
ANIMAL INSTINCT	50
REACTIONS TO FEELINGS AND FEELINGS ABOUT REACTIONS	51
PLEASE DON'T POISON THE WELL	52
THE CHILD LEFT	53
IN LIGHT OF EVERYTHING	54
CONSCIOUSNESS TAKEN TO HEART	55
OPENING DOORS	56
NOTHING TO FEAR	57
ON LOVE & DEATH	58
THINKING OF LEAVING	59
THE NEW ME	60
PARADOXICAL PEOPLE	61
THISTLE HOLLOW	62
LEARNING TO DANCE WHILE READING	63
HELLO OUT THERE!	64
DIRECTIONS FOR FINDING BEAUTY, TRUTH AND LOVE	65
PURPOSE	66

WRITTEN TRANSPORTATION	67
SMALL TOWN DOG	68
ALL FLIGHTS LEAD TO HOME	69
ACTORS IN MOVING PICTURES	70
CHAIN OF DIRECTION	71
DAYLIGHT AT THE END OF THE TUNNEL	72
DEPRESSION OBSESSION	73
EVIDENCE OF THE THOUGHT PROCESS	74
WHY TRY?	75
ASSASSINS OF OUR FUTURE (THE BULLET)	76
RESOLUTION	77
A MIRROR IS MORE THAN ITS SURFACE	78
ACCEPTING WHO I AM	79
YOU; US; I	80
WE ARE NOT SUNK YET	81
LIFE TIME	82
WE, YOU AND I	83
THE RACE TO SLOW DOWN	84
THE PROPER USE OF MOTION	85
THE MESSAGE IN THE MANIFESTATION OF LOVE	86
ABOUT THE POET	87

About the Book

On April 4th, 1999, I received a call from my wife saying that my father had died that morning. I was looking out over the Chesapeake Bay from the entrance to the Sassafras River. It was Easter Sunday, a beautiful Spring day, and I felt what seemed like a sonic boom that crossed over The Farm and out across the Bay. I was standing in my favorite place in my life, looking out over my favorite view. I could not have picked a better place to hear the news of my father's death. I looked out and said the words: "I'm in a beautiful place", and I didn't know if it referred to me or to my father; if it was my father or I who was speaking. He had been confined to bed for the last four years after undergoing an operation to remove a brain tumor. He never complained, only to tell us if he was hot or cold, or to respond: "I love you, too". He was loved and cared for by my mother for the entire time, transforming her from a scared woman faced with a daunting task into my father's primary caregiver.

I spent the next 5 hours or so walking on the beach at The Farm and thinking about my father, and Life, and then I began to realize that my mother had been given the day off, that the caregivers had been given Easter Sunday off; that my sister who had worked daily to keep my parents together till the very end, (They were both there at the moment of dad's death), was given the day off. Then, I realized that I no longer had to feel the guilt of not doing enough for him, effectively giving me the day off as well. It was the end of a long trial for my father and he, too, was given the day off from his patient struggle.

This book is written primarily since his death and I feel as if he should be named as a co-author. His influence in these pieces may be greater than mine, his example the motivation to write, his love expressed in these poems; his optimism in the face of hardship conveyed to others as an alternative to defeat.

Love is the opening door;

Love is what we came here for;

Do you know what I mean?

Have your eyes really seen?

~ Elton John

To My Father, Who Walked Into Heaven

Easter Sunday, April 4th, 1999
(Slightly After the First Guy)

My Father can be everywhere now that he is free
From the chains that held him here on Earth and he has taken me.
Through eyes that spoke his silence was a virtue.
There was no need to talk- his life said all.
When he was gone his presence just exploded:
"I'm in a beautiful place..."
You see, I know, I took the call.

So I joined him just because it was so easy,
In Beauty I reside as I write this;
For he showed us how to live within the moment
And there's no one who is gone for me to miss.
My Father guides my hand and takes me gently through the day;
I could almost walk with eyes closed
But he won't have things that way.

He's my star that shines out of the heavens
But he touches people still this day on Earth;
I used to question God: "Why am I here?"
His answer: "It's a miracle called "birth."
My Father lived each day;
Awoke to see what could be done
And of all the lives that he has touched-
I'm one.

So I will give you one small Truth to carry in your Heart,
My Father knew what he should do and the best day to depart.

Two Free Secrets Inside!

I hide my thoughts in poems
So thieves don't steal my dreams;
Idealists are subject to
Ridicule, it seems.

I keep my aspirations
Beneath a hardened shell,
Someday I'll let them out to play
But for now I hide them well.

People will rob you of your self-esteem
And then drive off with nary a wave;
Secretly I know that they are just here
Teaching me how to behave.

I can ignore truth and kindness,
I can steal peace of mind from a friend
But this is not why I was placed here
Nor the message God wants me to send.

When I was little I shared toys and treats,
I was taught it is best to be kind;
I should remember those two simple treasures
And hide them inside of these lines.

The Books of Life

I turn a page and my world expands;
My horizons increase with each word.
Every letter, blank space, drop of ink; pen to paper,
Serve as Songs from the Ages to be heard.

It would not be "True Life" if our Purpose was death,
We would "leave" through our own hand or Fate;
If Existence is meaningless why make the sun rise
And what End would Purpose create?

Faith holds the answer, the cure, the release,
One truly dies when they lack Love and Peace;
Self-serving matters are weights on one's Soul
But free will is the method where Mind takes control.

I am; therefore I can; therefore "I will" becomes the theme.
My thoughts are only limited by what I've heard and seen;
Eyes and ears are the portals to Mind and like books,
When one opens them up it will change how Life looks.

One Minute Meditation

Close you eyes and count three breaths,
Inhale… Exhale… That's one;
You must do two…to get to three…
But for now your work is done.

Let Mind conceive an atom,
Its molecular form if you will;
While moving at speeds that would make your head spin
To the eye objects seem to stand still.

Everything is in motion from the atom to the stars,
Eternal Motion does not sleep nor pause;
From the smallest to the largest
Balanced Movement is The Law.

You are in the perfect place,
All flaws are fleeting thoughts
And fear is just the need for Love,
Regardless of what you were taught.

Count three breaths and then open your eyes,
Inhale…molecular air,
Exhale…and let go, you awake when you know
A truth that has always been there.

Sit!

This morning my dog was chasing her tail,
Around and around she went;
Finally tired, she sat down
Quite happy and content.

And people are like that in one respect,
They feel like they're chasing their tail;
Around they race in an effort to face
The challenge of Life's next travail.

But things would be so much nicer,
We'd be in a better place
If we tired ourselves in happy contentment
During and after the race.

Sit down and spend a moment in the present,
Be the dog, enjoy the chases, too;
There's beauty in the second and this instant,
Enough to carry everybody through.

Songbirds in Spring at Daybreak

I have today in front of me
As daylight drifts into the trees;
Songbirds tired from their flight
Sing goodbye to one more night.

The sun hides just off to the East,
Waiting to appear;
Perhaps the songbird sings
Because a day of rest is near.

Songbirds migrate in the dark,
Alighting in city streets and parks;
It doesn't matter why they sing.
I listen for the joy they bring.

Old Information

Ancient scrolls were hidden in caves
Or secret sunken rooms;
Words of wisdom were written on walls
Within the Pharaohs' tombs.

Freedom from suffering defines the quest
Eternally sought till we're laid to rest;
Purpose in life leads to being aware
Of the suffering of ourselves and those in our care.

Compassion is freeing, it lets us relate;
Personal pain is an optional state.
Giving of self is just lending a hand;
All else is illusion created by Man.

Freedom and Human Rights

Peace of Mind constitutes Mans' Human Rights,
We all are entitled to calm;
There is no need to clench fists and be greedy,
We hold our fate in our palm.

If I believe I am better than you,
"You deserve less" is what I am saying;
I should think of my values, my time on this planet
And the message that I am conveying.

Build a warm fire against Winter's chill,
In the Springtime the fields fill with flowers;
Summer and Fall are the best times of all,
Count the treasures of Time by their hours.

Fall into freedom by loving yourself,
You're unique if you think you are so;
Love is contagious but only through contact,
It's your choice and I thought you should know.

It Takes an Eternity to Get to This Second

Nothing lasts forever;
Each second comes and goes.
Why would we think of holding on?
Heaven only knows.

All indicators point to one conclusion
And that is that clinging just adds to confusion;
Let go of all things, both views and possessions,
Actions and motives then leave clear impressions.

In between our ears we think,
Our eyes are the filters of light,
Perception is the melting pot
In the miracle of Life.

Nothing lasts forever;
Harsh acts often try
To outlast Love but Love wins out
As Perfection passes by.

Experience Only, Please!

My goal is to experience,
Nothing more or less;
When I begin to analyze
It seems that I digress.

I place two words together
And facts begin to blur;
"I am", "I think" and other quips
Like these sometimes occur.

My goal is just to watch the world
As it goes spinning by;
I can't conceive totality,
It makes no sense to try.

My hope is that one day I'll be
Satisfied with being me,
Maybe happy just by chance
And hearing the music, I begin to dance.

Speaking of Silence

Like the Sphinx I am stuck
As the hourglass funnels
The Future and Present to Past,
Staring in wonder, one blink and I'm History;
Neither bad, good nor Now ever lasts.

Inertia spins gyroscopes in one direction,
Force is required to change
But please remember it also takes effort
Or work if we wish to maintain.

Movement and stillness are as Fear and Faith,
Immovable objects combined
With irresistible forces,
Then distilled within each Mind.

Silently thinking or speaking out loud,
I am Sphinx-like, a mystery in Time
But these words are the difference;
Speech conveys Love
And our actions are movement defined.

Putting Music to Words

These are the words to the music inside
Each Soul as it comes into form,
Harmony lives in the cell and each center;
Calm exists in the eye of the storm.

Songs of the Universe already sung
Transfer the Wisdom from old folks to young.
Youth turns to Wise Man, his beard turns to gray;
In passing we change lives and a part of us stays.

What we turn into God only knows.
We get to learn more as consciousness grows.
I hear the music, it stirs from within;
One dance must end for the next to begin.

Movement is motion divinely inspired,
Love is constant through Cosmos and each
Soul that aspires to fan ember to fire,
Learn the music, hear the message- of Peace.

Picture Perfect

I carry pictures around in my head
But they're common so I take no heed;
Recessed into stillness they sleep until called up,
I retrieve them as I feel the need.

All of the actions, events that I've seen,
Are recorded and filed quite neatly;
Light carries images out into space
And fills in the colors completely.

I often develop opinions and views
Through the clouded lens of misperception;
Hopelessness, sadness, despair and aloneness
Wither upon close inspection.

There is no reason to fear things I see,
They happen then turn into mist;
Like pages in scrapbooks we move in a timeline,
It's just the way humans exist.
Picture yourself as Perfect;
Confluent, Complete, Content,
Happy with self and others
As the decades came and went.

The Beauty of Perception

Beauty is as beauty does,
It always will be and it always was;
Some things change and all things do,
Innovative thinking is nothing new.

As concept embraces perception,
Love holds beauty within its confines
But what would this mean if it were not for you,
The vessel that carries your Mind?

Think what you're doing but act nonetheless,
Creation implies demonstration;
Look to yourself as a miracle manifest,
Focused energy of God's direction.

Purpose and Beauty are only defined
By the brain that's in contact with Mind.
What will you do with this thing that's called "you"
And what are you hoping to find?

Purpose gives Meaning as Beauty is seen.
In the eye you behold and perceive.
I am also a part of some Cosmic Convergence;
We are Beauty, or so I believe.

Think what you will, it's your choice don't you know,
But the Source of each thought has decided
To leave Love as a signpost, with Spirit as Guide
For the journey occurring inside us.

Cosmic Chicken Soup

The mystery of Life is such
That what a person eats
Becomes a body of itself
In a cycle that repeats.

I take in an orange after peeling the skin,
Savoring sweetness and smell;
Cool juices quench thirst, the seeds go on saucers
As I become nourished as well.

Fruits of our labor give sustenance, too,
They define composition of Soul;
We are in need of a Source to maintain us
As Body and Spirit made whole.

We ingest food, we take in Life,
This Life is the record we leave;
Then the Universe is kind enough
To confirm what the Mind perceives.

Are We Immortal Or Eternal?

Immortality implies that we keep
On living after we die;
While the word "eternal" may be defined
As before we were born we had a mind.

Death is a process that Spirit goes through,
One chapter in volumes of books;
In spite of how Man may see himself,
He is never the way he looks.

Prior to stories of angels and ghosts
We were "here" and then "there" all the time;
All the illusion and mental confusion
Are tricks Humans play on their Mind.

If I think of myself or my Life as a void
It may very well prove to be true;
To decide I am lonely, sad, empty or broken
Is defining small scenes as grand views.

Everyone tends to get side-tracked by thinking
That being alive is a chore;
When I stop for ten seconds to look for my purpose
I find Life can have meaning and more.

Love, support and compassion for stranger or friend
Becomes instant Self-gratification;
I am grateful and changed as the Cosmos unwraps
The gift of eternal Creation.

Before you were born you were well on your way,
Spirit preceding arrival;
When you leave I will see you again in True Form
For the Soul is designed for survival.

Fixing Everything

When will the whole world decide to choose Peace,
Is the blood shed through violence a joke;
If things work we don't fix them but why can't we see
That a Mind ruled by anger is broken?

Hateful reactions implode on themselves
As the victim becomes the abuser
Or whole families rise up, revenge starts anew
And the Innocent turns to accuser.

Pieces and parts are what make up the whole,
From the atom to Cosmic Convergence;
Why spin in discord as The Universe waits
For a peaceful solution's emergence?

We are the problem, the whole world is broken;
Let's fix what we can 'till we're done.
Nothing's impossible once we're aware
Of the blessings when Mankind means One.

Evolution Solution

Kind acts hold power to change someone's Life,
Mean acts affect folks as well;
I can recall unconditional Love,
There are also sad stories I could tell.

People will pick you up when you are down,
The Empath halts in his stride
To change two perspectives, his own and another's;
Affecting not one but two lives.

But the robber who takes what he thinks he deserves
Because someone left him somehow lacking
Will become his own victim for all things are equal,
It is their own self-esteem they are attacking.

Thief or Samaritan, which shoe fits you?
We are perfect reflections of what we say and do.
Pass by the homeless, the hungry, lost Soul;
At your core you'll be digging your own little hole.

Now for the kind act: "There's no one to blame",
Cause and consequence yield evolution;
Ignorance is merely Truth's patient waiting
For us to provide the solution.

The Perception of Peace

Peace is just five letters,
Two consonants, three vowels;
The word contains a wealth of weight
Yet we treat it lightly, somehow.

All the world argues
That their war is just
Or that compromise weakens
And fosters mistrust.

Non-aggression is an action,
Not an act of standing still;
Retaliation makes no friends
And resentment never will.

Doing right in spite of instinct
Brings the battle down to size;
The mind that sits between my ears
Must learn to compromise.

Meeting in the middle
With hands instead of arms
Or fighting to find common ground
Seldom does much harm.

There are winners and losers in each interaction
If life means we simply keep score
But if I have no peace or don't know what the word means
Then I don't know what I'm here for.

Being Here Now

It's a chore to remain in the moment,
I can't be Here all of the time;
Outside influences mesmerize me,
Worldly affairs fill my mind.

While sitting alone my thoughts wander,
I am distracted by crowds;
My own voice tends to confuse me
When I speak opinions out loud.

Cell phones ring out or the message light blinks,
I'm held captive by comments and what others think;
Being Here Now is a consummate chore
But the Body Soul lives in is hard to ignore.

I can exist in the present
If I focus and don't let thoughts stray;
Past acts and future fears fall to the side
When I simply live in today.

Planting the Seed

When I dig in the garden I uncover Faith;
I believe plants and flowers will grow.
Sometime this Summer, perhaps in Fall, too,
If I'm lucky I'll reap what I sow.

While removing the weeds from the garden out back
I can think as I work hands and feet;
They all move in confluence as I prune perspectives
On how I will act should we meet.

Pick out a patch, a small place of your own,
With the changing of seasons, see how you've both grown;
Labor and Love are too often confused
By warped or mistaken thinking and views.

Work with your hands and your Mind tags along,
Spring, Summer, Fall, Winter will come and be gone
But you now hold the seed and the faith it will grow.
In both Spirit and garden we reap as we sow.

Which Came First, the Chicken Or the Eggestential Concept?

Regardless of whether I'm here for a Purpose
Or not is a matter of view;
Others debate the same subject with fervor,
Each believing one perspective to be true.

But perhaps Truth is bigger than one Mind perceives
Unless One Mind is defined as the whole;
Like a spoonful of honey stirred mixes with morning tea
Ours is one of many Sacred Souls.

Sunrise falls equally, none are denied,
Dawn is a new day on Earth;
Whether we're here for a Purpose or not
Every day is a Gift of re-birth.

Love is the secret to being alive
In the literal and the abstract;
Consciousness is merely caring for all,
Not some litany of things that I lack.

I Am; therefore I can; therefore I will becomes the mantra,
Notice how Nature nurtures our Universe;
As constellations shed Light on the Grand Illumination
Love and Purpose rule Supreme and must come first.

Train of Thought

Life is a train that we're passengers on,
The scenery slides by as we stand.
Still we have movement within these confines.
Isn't the paradox grand?

Choice is a matter of free will
But how can one learn without loss;
Why would we choose to be grateful
If nothing had meaning or cause?

Look out the window as Life passes by;
The Present turns Past in the wink of an eye.
Now is the instant and Effort is action,
Love is our destiny; all else distraction.

Gifts and Presence

Kindness is a gift
That does not come with cards and bows,
There is no need to wrap up help
With strings or demands that grow.

I am not required
To make a windy speech;
The motives that I might reveal
I may not want to teach.

Unwrap the gifts that your Life has presented,
Let go of hatred that you have invented;
Peace is a possible alternative
To the hurried existence with which humans live.

Inhale Life and breathe out peace,
Compassion's in the air;
Emotion and action will mix and mingle
When the gift of your presence is there.

Activities Performed Without Moving

I sense stillness in the early hours
When darkness sits with silence for a bit;
A firefly stops by and after visiting my hand,
Launches from my upright fingertip.

Quiet moments form a chain
Link, by link, by link;
Meditation, books and writing
Stretch the way I think.

Mind and Body seek the peace
That stillness lights upon;
I move within and then without
To greet the new day's dawn.

Stillness and movement are never apart,
They exist symbiotically in Soul and Heart;
Like Sunrise and Sunset are both in one day
I carry stillness in moveable ways.

Voice Lessons

Thought is conscience speaking,
Spirit asking for attention;
Our response then varies
According to intention.

Cover your ears and hum,
Refuse to hear those Inner Words;
Pretend there is no substance
And you'll get what you deserve.

The Universal Law agrees with all
Of our emotions;
Denial is acceptable
And so is true devotion.

Clean your house and your side of the street.
Show respect, each Soul you meet
Contains the spark of God and good
When Spirit is heard and understood.

Thought is conscience speaking,
Listen and take heed;
Compassion is the key to Love
And Love is all we need.

Inside/Out

I know I have an outside, as anyone can see;
It's visible from head to toe, I like to call it: "Me".
I must include the thoughts I have,
They are critically crucial as well
And all of my inner parts are required
Or else I would just be a shell.

There are atoms galore that I need to survive;
Electrons and protons help keep me alive.
My heart tells my head, through transmitters it's said,
Of emotions I sometimes go through;
Then my head tells my heart that in stillness I start
And in silence I find what is true.

My outside walks around, it lets me move from "Here" to "There"
While the inside simply follows- they're the perfectly matched pair.
An inner and an outer self merge and become as one;
They comprise the better part of me when all is said and done.

Return to Center

Be kind to your thoughts and feelings,
They make up the Mind and Soul;
Reflect upon your gentle side
And let it take control.

Progress has never been defined
As an action that crushes or steals peace of mind;
Rudeness was never described as a virtue
And acts that hurt Humans return and then haunt you.

Save yourself trouble, invest all your time
Dreaming up ways to be gentle and kind.
Place yourself right in the middle
Of all that Life holds out to Man
And remember kindness changes two lives
Every time you say it can.

One Life

I become timeless if I leave a mark
On more than just one Human heart;
Yet I must focus on that one
Suffering soul who has come undone.

People fall and get back up
A million times a day;
It never is the fall that hurts,
It's the pain in which we lay.

Sooner or later my body will pass,
There to find heaven or that nothing lasts
But in the meantime, until it's: "light's out",
Folks interacting is what Life's about.

Choice Decisions

My passing through leaves not a trace
And the dust of Time conceals
All but the things we say or do
Or make another feel.

Act on anger, lose a friend,
Sit alone at your wits end;
Hold a grudge, refuse to budge
And see how well Man mends.

A rut is just a retrogressive groove,
Our choice is to stay stuck or else improve;
As we spin the wheels of negativity
Throwing mud will never get us free.

Ask someone to help you out
Of the pit of anger, confusion or doubt
Or throw a rope to some poor soul;
As we lose self we gain control.

Caring doesn't cost one cent,
Compassion often is free;
The price that we pay for what we do and say
Determines your value to me.

Don't Be Afraid to Think about What You Know

The downfall of Man was arrogance
And not The Tree of Knowledge,
We killed the messenger but not the cause;
Stories change the details,
Turn the finer points to mist,
We magnify or minimize our flaws.

Abundance is more than enough to sustain,
Infinity can't be corralled,
Happiness shared becomes Love overflowing;
Voice is Spirit speaking out loud.

What I say matters; what I do will last,
My actions today become part of my past.
In this instant is movement, all else introspection;
Wisdom passed down provides all my direction.

Kind acts hold weight; Love has function and form,
Mind perceives and then reaches its goal.
We transcend the distractions through unified Love,
Merging Body, Mind, Spirit and Soul.

Adam and Eve were just like you and me,
They were crushed by their ego
Not snake, apple nor tree;
The Wisdom of Ages is the ladder Thought climbs,
There's no need for aversion to using your Mind.

Human Emotions

Sad stories should not make me weep,
Grown men should not cry;
Books are simply words on pages
Filtered through my eyes.

Neurotransmitters are how doctors label
What makes our brain work and keeps our thoughts stable
But there are more than just neurons involved
Leading to where humankind has evolved.

Emotions are feelings that hold cosmic weight,
Compassion and empathy help us relate;
Anger is energy, progress reversed,
Exposing our defects when we're at our worst.

Sad stories move me, sometimes I cry,
Beauty as well brings a tear to my eye;
Human emotion is destined to be
Contained inside people just like you and me.

Compassion as an Alternative

Abuse leaves scars that never heal
Although one thinks they do;
Physical or verbal,
They affect what we go through.

Torture is bodily pain inflicted
Or mental distress without end;
Feelings of powerlessness breed despair.
Once we're broken it's harder to bend.

Helplessness makes holes in trust,
Erases self-esteem;
Abuse will grow and multiply
Then kill our hopes and dreams.

Look to Compassion;
It won't heal the scar
But it may redefine us
And change who we are.

Choice Encounter

Choice is a word that holds power;
Just six letters, three consonants, three vowels
But it holds both our past and future
And defines what we're doing right now.

Positive actions are as we perceive,
Environment influences what we believe;
I'm at the center of choices I make,
You, too, have your own life and path you must take.

I choose to make good choices just for today,
When I go out this morning I'll watch what I say;
To be calm in a cruel world takes patience combined
With a choice to be gentle, loving and kind.

Alternatives

What is the purpose of Life without joy
Or glimpses of Peace now and then?
I cannot remember when tension and strain,
The concept that growth requires pain,
Overtook us.

Why are we here in this valley of tears;
Who said this was our destination?
The Sun seems to rise, bringing light to our lives
And the seasons imply restoration.

Peace can be part of our daily routine,
Love is a two-way street;
Life is renewed at the break of the day,
Reaffirmed every time kind folks meet.

Evolving Ideals

Love can't be held unless given away.
Strength and Peace are decisions we make.
Roots are required for flowers to bloom;
And this garden is ours' to create.

Something greater than my self
Forms while I observe
That existence can only occur as it happens
But our thoughts may be calm or disturbed.

Therefore my thinking reflects where I've been,
Mind will project and adjust;
Life is Divine Signature giving proof
Of a Universe made just for us.

All we are given was ours all along.
What is here has existed since time.
Only the choice as to how we move through Life
Turns from History into Evolution of our Minds.

Confluence

The physical mimics the spiritual world,
Facts will confirm the Divine;
Locks that are opened
Or walls we remove
Are mental directional signs.

Gravity proves we are grounded,
There's air for the whole world to breathe;
One would assume there is Love all around
And more Hope than the Human race needs.

Anger's Obituary

I killed anger yesterday,
We had an awful fight;
He claimed that he was justified
But I'd read that's never right.

Anger is cunning, it seeks to deceive
And enjoys when you fight with a friend;
Everyone loses when anger wins out—
Yet we go back and do it again.

I figure fights should be chosen with care,
Sometimes mountains are molehills disguised;
Killing our anger pulls weeds at their roots
And allows us to lead happy lives.

Time Changes

Positive attitudes come and go,
Like the tides they move in and then leave,
Often our highest dreams crumble to dust;
We forget or are crushed when deceived.

Peace of mind stumbles and falls upon lies,
Happiness dies on the vine;
Losses occur on the path all Souls walk
But the pain dissipates in due time.

Sooner or later the smile will return,
After night we are blessed with the dawn.
Time changes negatives back into positives.
Clouds hide the Sun then move on.

Please don't stay stuck in the rut of despair,
Help is on the way;
Kind acts, compassion and laughter
Have simply been delayed.

Animal Instinct

The way in which I treat my pets
 Reveals my frame of mind;
To some degree they depend on me,
 It's how we are defined.

If I snap or bark,
If I should scratch you when we pass,
Please excuse my being rude,
My house is made of glass.

Anger is a silly thought; it makes no sense to me
And yet I seem to wrestle with my anger frequently.
The better course has always been to scratch the place we itch;
Our pets can teach us many things, two of these are which:

My pets tend to make me think,
I try to stay ahead;
And watch those thoughts
That mouse-like race
On the wheels inside my head.

Reactions to Feelings and Feelings about Reactions

I watch my cat traverse the room,
It simply is a cat
But I lose my mind if he climbs the drapes,
I won't put up with that.

When I'm perturbed I become disturbed,
The two may form a link
But they are different,
Reactions show; feelings are what I think.

How we feel determines our reaction,
We give praise or else conversely pass out blame;
Regardless of opinions that may form and fade like fog,
Thoughts and actions never are the same.

Please Don't Poison the Well

The days drop by like butterflies,
They alight and then move on;
A replication of perfection
Starting with each dawn.

The Sun comes up, the stage is set;
Enjoy the show, it's free.
Trees are cleaning up the place
For the likes of you and me.

But unkind acts and vicious words
Destroy the set and scene;
It only takes one harmful move
To cloud or kill a dream.

Please don't poison the well of Peace;
If you are angry perhaps you could cease.
Depression and fear are destructive illusion;
Kind acts and Love are the perfect solution.

The Child Left

Because I did not learn when asked
It seems I must repeat the past.
The Indian on a vast green plain
Laughs at my plight, reveals my pain.

He must have felt an ache within
The center of his being;
To watch the disregard for Earth
But unable to change what he's seeing.

Now I get to watch the land abused,
The forest battered, the mountains bruised,
The air polluted, my streams diluted-
My whole world changing; my Being uprooted.

But a spirited Pioneer crossing the Plain,
Seeing valleys and mountains too numerous to name,
Passes by an old Indian sitting alone
In helpless confusion; his heart like a stone.

In Light of Everything

If birds did not sing as the stars fade at dawn,
If a firefly never left home,
If we've spent our lives hiding from the Gift of Abundance
We run risks of feeling alone.

Interaction means listening to birds as they sing,
Holding the notes in your Mind;
On the tip of my finger a firefly lights,
Sound and Light are two ways Life's defined.

Love is another vibration we see,
One we feel to the goose bumps we get;
Love experienced sheds Light on paths where we act right
And History is the record we have left.

Down through vast eons as planets were formed,
As the stars took their hold on the sky,
Time passed time looking out into the Future
Until Mind formed the question: "Why?"

Why do I think I am not of the stars
Or a part of a songbird at dawn?
By the light of each day I am learning my place;
I'll leave footprints long after I'm gone.

Death is not death in the Great Scheme of Things,
All signs indicate we're All right;
Constellations have patiently turned till your time
Changes darkness to concepts of Light.

Consciousness Taken to Heart

Consciousness is what we know,
It makes us who we are;
We trudge through ruts of mind and muck
Or dance among the stars.

Attitude defines our life,
While motives make the man;
The total of our actions
Sum up just where we stand.

Faith forms a self-imposed level,
Fear is a fable minds tell;
Consciousness is the result of our deeds,
We construct our own heaven or hell.

Consciousness requires time,
The journey is one small part;
Events are filtered through our thoughts
Then settle in our heart.

Opening Doors

I open the door to compassion,
Empathy serves as the key;
Nothing exists or has meaning
That somehow does not affect me.

Frogs, squirrels and bumblebees all play a part
In the dance and the whirl of existence;
Movement of Soul is a part of the whole
Here to teach me through constant persistence.

Closed doors are like walls, they are hard to go through
But an open door tends to enhance
Views and horizons and may bring more light
Or allow Self to slowly advance.

The planets don't tilt to demands I may make,
Rather it's I that must bend
To the will of the force that created all life forms,
For I'm just the means to an end.

I touch the world and the world touches me,
I walk through doors and into perceptions.
Frogs, squirrels and bumblebees form little links;
It is I that must make the connections.

Nothing to Fear

Fear always comes from an outside source
But distills itself in my mind
Unless I am focused, patient and tolerant,
Self-restrained, mindful and kind.

My Fear is always followed by my anger;
One stokes the fire; one the bellows mans.
The two wreak havoc with friends and relations
And frustrate all my well-intentioned plans.

Like ants I follow trails to where they lead me;
There's a picnic at the end of one, I know,
With cake and ice cream for my Soul and Spirit
If I am willing to relax and grow.

But if Fear is what turns all my gears
And blocks the paths between my ears,
I'll never sit and feel the glow
That those at Peace have come to know.

On Love & Death

When someone that I love is taken by the hand of death
I have the option to despair, to move through life bereft.
Death can break the bond between two kindred spirit souls;
Demise can grasp our lofty thoughts and shoot them full of holes.

Death is the actress who lowers the veil,
Who closes the door or fills our sail;
But when a door closes one would assume
It is simply a threshold to some other room.

When folks are alive and walking about
Is the best time to love them and work problems out
Because when they are gone we can't change what we've done
Or express that two spirits have traveled as one.

Thinking of Leaving

Leaving the room does not mean I have died,
I am not here so that might be implied;
Why would we think that when Spirit moves on
Nothing remains or what was here is gone?

Energy can't be destroyed, it may change;
If nothing matters then that would be strange.
Souls that incarnate are here for a reason;
Death is transition like cycles of seasons.

Winter is cold and then Spring colors in,
Greys and their shadows depart;
Summer's warm rays and Fall leaves on display
Portray endings as simply new starts.

Leaving a room means that I may return,
Don't lock the door to your mind;
Keep open options, move through confusion,
Have Faith, Love Self and be kind.

The New Me

A different person greets each day
As I rise out of bed;
Yesterday's me has come and gone,
A new person lives in my head.

A day that has passed does not define
Your Life or for that matter mine;
The seconds gone are just a blur,
Lines converge and the spheres concur.

My perception changes, too,
On how I tend to look at you;
Friend or foe, rose or thorn,
I judge on substance, style and form.

In spite of all the evidence,
When each new day arrives
I start off injecting my judgments
And listening to all of my lies.

But tomorrow I'm turning a new leaf,
I'll be new when these lines have been read;
Please respond if inclined in some fashion
To these musings on past lives I've led.

Paradoxical People

People that I don't like
Really are my friends;
It may seem strange but
They make me change-
A paradoxical means to an end.

Slap me with an open hand
Or say mean words because you can;
You are no more than some stimuli
When you act rude as you go by.

I get to see what's right and wrong,
I confirm the values I've held all along;
I do not pay a karmic toll
By learning through another soul.

Thistle Hollow

I go to Thistle Hollow in the mountains,
Dragonflies zig-zag through noonday sun
And just before days end or at its dawning
I find is when the smallmouth tend to run.

I see a mouse with corn-fed rear
Cross the cupboard, then disappear.
I would have thrown him from the house
Were he not such a crafty mouse.
He hid until the stars came out,
When crickets chirp and hop about.

A deer stands just beside the shed,
Two does reveal their lop-eared heads;
They do not try to run and hide,
From Greg... or the dog...on point...
by my side.

Learning to Dance while Reading

It is my reading, as well as my doing
Which improves my state of mind;
I can read about how great life is
But my actions are how I'm defined.

We dance or crawl, we stand and fall
As the cosmic clock unwinds;
Seconds and minutes flow into Lifetimes
And Life is the true tie that binds.

From birth till tomb we are consumed
While we emanate Life and Light.
The miracle of being Here
Is the source of our Delight.

Love is the signal as to how one should act.
Common sense leads the horse to take drink.
Both the mule and the racehorse accept what they are
And are set in the ways that they think.

I can read books while I'm running this race.
I can go fast or slow or get stuck in one place,
Then along comes a thought set in print that I read
Which says Love is a dance and perhaps I should lead.

Hello Out There!

I waved to you as I went by,
As another camera caught my eye
And I will never be alone,
Now that they can tap my phone.

I stopped to buy some milk and then –
My face smiled back with where and when;
A time - stamped record followed by an ad,
Retrievable by keyboard if I'm bad.

The Bank said: "No!" to my request
To withdraw my hard-earned cash-
There's a note attached to my receipt
That says my eyes don't match.

I know it's all for my own good,
That there still is seclusion deep in the woods;
But I have to walk the dog today-
I'll be sure to wave along the way.

Directions for finding Beauty, Truth and Love

I seek Truth, I find Truth,
I find Love and love
Or Beauty eludes me and then–
A flower, a picture, some joke or a friend
Brings the colors of Life back again.

When I don't see the world in its glory,
For the oceans, sunrise or sunset
Perhaps I should shuffle myself to a place
Where my Soul and its Source can connect.

Even to open a gift takes some work,
Desire and movement makes form;
Peace will not barge in, it waits at the door
And has called since the Cosmos was born.

Truth does not run from the Bully of Lies,
Beauty springs forth every year;
There is Love for the asking and Faith, when I touch Faith
Removes false aloneness and fear.

I think I'll accept this world's blessings,
Love, Beauty and Truth may be found
Within myself, in you; in all
If I just look around.

Purpose

I often take a single fact
And turn it into two;
I complicate what's simple
By inserting my own view.

Things are one until I get
My hands into the mix;
I analyze and then decide
Which parts of Life to fix.

The little wheels of ego
And my self-centered pride
Roll around between my ears
Before they go outside.

I am not in charge of every
Star nor bird that flies;
I do not place the spark of Life
Behind a pair of eyes.

My role is rather limited,
And yet I have a place,
When I temper life with Loving
I join the Human Race.

Written Transportation

Poetry is enchanting,
The Fairies fly with ink;
My Mind creates my hopes and dreams
Then I write down what I think.

Poems convey compassion,
Poets bleed on the page;
Words can release or entrap you,
Set one free or place folks in a cage.

I would suggest reading words that give flight,
Books about wings, clouds and wheels;
Lightness and movement exist in the moment,
Reading will change how one feels.

I go to Paris or live in the woods,
I touch clouds or dive into the sea,
Poets proclaim Love in volumes of verses;
This is how writing should be.

Small Town Dog

The city in which I grew up
Had some neighbors with a dog
Who wandered far and wide each night;
All nose and tail and paws.

People said he used the stars
To navigate his way;
He would come home right at daybreak
And sleep throughout the day.

The sight of the late night delivery truck,
The hiss of the tires of cars,
The swaying of trees in the 2 a.m. breeze,
Traveling; watching the stars.

Everyone liked that doggie,
He was known and loved all over town;
It's a shame that today things are not the same way,
He'd be hunted and put in the pound.

Perhaps today we're all mongrels,
Guilty of invented sin
But I like the idea of freedom
To follow the stars and the wind.

All Flights Lead To Home

A butterfly landed upon my shirt
As I walked along the Bay;
I lifted him up on my finger to fly
But my Monarch decided to stay.

I saw his tiny Monarch tongue
Reach out and touch me on my thumb;
Under a shimmering summer sun
For just a moment we are one.

There's a story I've heard that in China
The beating of butterfly wings
Moves the air that's around it
And thus affects all things.

I took my little butterfly
And we gave that theory the college try;
Sure enough he moved the air
Made by trees right over there,
The breeze touched the river that leads to the Bay
Where a butterfly brightens
My sweet Summer day.

Actors in Moving Pictures

Learning does not hurt once it is tucked
into the mind;
It's hard to recollect the pain
of trials left behind.

Pain is real, it's all we feel
When things come much too fast;
Yet true growth is a fact as well,
Affirmed once pain has passed.

Growth and pain are see-saw games,
We learn through fits and starts
To dance upon a cosmic stage
And play the perfect part.

Chain of Direction

We are Divine links that form chains in Time
Stretching out in all directions;
Consciously focus from right where you are
On subtle yet concrete connections.

Everyone's linked to each other,
Admit or deny them that place;
Even the beggar, homeless and friendless,
Fills up a valuable space.

People and Nature form a chain,
One fragile echo-system;
The air we breathe, the soil and seed
Speak and we must listen.

Nothing is here forever.
Energy can't be destroyed.
But kind acts and Compassion
Link hearts and fill the voids.

Daylight at the End of the Tunnel

There's always Hope until there's not,
That seems to be the Human lot
And yet within the darkest night
Somewhere everything's all right.

When I'm sure that Life's not worth
The effort to remain on Earth
Somewhere darkness yields to dawn;
Perhaps I need to just move on.

What does it take to continue
Or to find Hope through trial and pain?
Perhaps it's to think that when times look the darkest
Daylight is coming again.

Depression Obsession

Depression comes when one feels bad
About their human side;
We stay in bed or in our head
While seeking just to hide.

The answer is the Self it seems,
When expectations rise from dreams;
If we're not happy where we are
We are looking down, not at the stars.

Raise your head and look around,
See in your mind what others have found;
Beyond the Self and Ego lies
A reality seen through other eyes.

The poor and the suffering, the calm and serene
Are catalysts for Life's lessons;
When combined with God's grace we soon begin
To lose our sad obsessions.

Evidence of the Thought Process

There's a difference between what one thinks and one's actions;
The first can move people, the latter moves mountains.
My thinking may get me where I want to go
But if there is no evidence, how will I know?

Thinking is great for it helps us resolve
The problems Life hands us when crises evolve;
Yet movement is necessary used in conjunction
With thoughts or else all is just mindless compunction.

Psychiatrists couches are filled with the masses
And millions have taken assertiveness classes;
There's yoga and tai-chi, we meditate some,
But unless there is action, those actions seem dumb.

If I'm deaf to the cries that provoke me to move,
Or blind to my faults and the guilt that intrudes,
My thoughts are just vapors that soon disappear
Unless action leaves evidence that they were here.

Why Try?

Effort is the secret force,
The key, the answer, more;
Effort is the sum effect
Of all that's come before.

Folks prepare us for the world,
We learn Life as we go-
But it's effort that is underlying;
Effort is how we grow.

Bugs make an effort to climb leaves and grass,
Grass makes an effort to bend as bugs pass,
Effort and triumph exist side by side;
We only reach mountaintops after we've tried.

Assassins of Our Future
(The Bullet)

Perhaps it lies upon some shelf
Or in a box, or drawer;
Innocent, sitting alone I should think
Just past the "Crime Evidence" door.

The room is dark, the lights are out,
A quiet cloak descends
Upon the grains of stoic lead
And hearts that cannot mend.

Kennedy, Oswald, Ruby,
Simply the names of three men.
Victim, Assassin, Avenger;
Lincoln and Martin again.
Silence fills the vacuum, hatred locks the door;
Hope dies to an ember, till the fire is lit once more.

How many times will Phoenix-like
The Human Race revive
The concept that all men are one
And tame our baser side?

How many times will Fate be left
In hands that hold no Hope;
They leave behind our hearts and minds
In a whisper of vanishing smoke.

Resolution

When I resolve a problem,
It simply goes away;
I'm free to set about the chores
That challenge me each day.

If I drag around a problem
Or wear it on my face,
The world gets smaller as my mind
Creates a lesser space.

Thinking about a problem
Makes me shiver to my toes,
I don't tolerate pain well at all;
And avoidance attracts me, God knows.

So I'll ask someone to help me out
Of this hole I've fallen in;
I reach out as an imperfect Human
Who is searching for Peace within.

A Mirror Is More than Its Surface

I reflect the Light that comes
From a bulb in a room or the Sun;
I take in Light, I give off Light,
It is just the way it's done.

Mirrors reflect to a certain degree
Clarity as well as flaws;
Polish the surface and all that's inside
Already contain Nature's Laws.

Reflection occurs on our insides as well;
Our thought process defines Self through Mind.
It takes all of what's in us to shine on the outside;
Nature's Laws dictate how we're designed.

I suppose I reflect what The Universe wants,
I am subject and object and link;
Only your Mind in conjunction with Nature
Reflects on the way that you think.

Reflections are images from other sources,
There never has been an exception;
Outside Light is required for Humans to thrive
And you're Nature is of Divine Conception.

Accepting Who I Am

I travel by car, foot, plane, train; Mind.
I arrive at perspectives and places.
Unless I remember or I am remembered
My passing leaves no traces.

Too many subjects can clutter the brain,
Long sentences sometimes cause sleep,
Boredom's a sign warning of unawareness;
What the Mind sows the Body shall reap.

Think what you will, it's true freedom instilled
To the center, that core of your Being;
Constellations are formed, you become the beholder
By accepting the Beauty you're seeing.

Views form perceptions; perceptions beliefs,
We arrive or fall short of the goal;
Mind is Perfect, inherent, alive in each atom.
There is nothing not part of The Whole.

Wander the Earth, read a book, sit in silence
But waste not, this instant defines
Movement and Progress, awareness; acceptance
Of our being one part Human, one part Divine.

You; Us; I

Concepts are not perfect,
Ideals are not facts,
Few things in life are pristine;
Sometimes the deck is stacked.

Simple things are complex
Or thoughts can make them so;
I find I know too little
And with that in mind, I grow.

Front and back are relevant
Only from two views;
Good and bad have shown me
That I am just like you.

There is a point to this poem,
I simply write down the lines;
They converge in these words
And I find it absurd
To think that your problems aren't mine.

We Are Not Sunk Yet

If all are perfect in God's eyes,
Then Mankind must be blind;
I fail to see perfection
When anyone's unkind.

Acting and speaking the part of the fool
Requires abandoning grace.
How do affirmatives come from self-centeredness;
Love from the depths of disgrace?

Out of despair falls a flicker of hope,
Perhaps Life's not as cold nor so cruel;
I touch perfection, I rise from the ashes
Simply by picking up tools.

Minds have been given to recognize trends,
Truth does not come in two sizes;
Love of all others as well as yourself
Occurs and perfection arises.

Maybe things are not as bad as they seem,
Kind acts are motives as form;
God knows perfection, we are mere vessels
Sheltered thus far from the storm.

Life Time

The present confirms the events of the past,
All moments merge into Here;
Future reality is the effect
Of creations we cause to appear.

Even free gifts require some work to unwrap,
It takes effort to get out of bed;
Showing small kindnesses means one has labored
To think with their heart *and* their head.

Pulsing vibrations, waves moving light,
Energy coursing through veins,
Planets are balanced in oceans of galaxies;
Thousands of eons remain.

Time is just light, we are part of our past,
Every second our future arrives;
Moments are precious and fleeting, reflecting
The depth and the breadth of our lives.

We, You and I

If anger is the symptom,
What is the disease?
Which malady controls the Mind
And makes us hard to please?

Please define your anger,
This will help you grow;
Compassion, love, and tolerance
Are actions, don't you know.

I am prone to anger
If I'm not treated right,
I ruminate and postulate;
I document my strife.

Why do we get angry?
It seems we demand our own way.
When we fail to respect another…
There's a cost that our self-esteem pays.

Anger is the symptom,
Pride the core disease;
Just remove false pride and deep inside
Hides the cure that we all need.

The Race to Slow Down

I can't find Serenity,
It seems to be avoiding me;
And when I am in Hot Pursuit -
I find it's on a different route.

I'm chasing after Peace of Mind;
It's something I must race to find.
The faster I go, the closer I get-
I can see it and taste it; I'm just not there yet.

Patience eludes me, I can't bear to wait,
To sit in the moment just means I'll be late;
So I'm asking for Patience, but I want it now-
Lord, give me Patience and I don't care how.

Serenity and Peace of Mind,
Patience and just being kind,
Require me to use the brakes;
Slow down or Stop, whichever it takes.

The Proper Use of Motion

When I've made the rounds on this mortal coil
And shuffle off from this scene
I do not wish to leave behind
Bad memories or broken dreams.

Self-centered, self-absorbed, wanting and greedy
Define actions forming a link
Or through peaceful, calm patience and untethered Love
I evolve into what my Mind thinks.

Motives plus motion make people alive,
In this moment is where all must live;
The Future is vision, our past is now history,
Leaving a record of what we take and what we give.

Like a drop of dew that slips into
A shining endless ocean,
I should hope my Life reflects good Luck
And Proper use of Motion.

The Message in the Manifestation of Love

Love is the bond of Perfection
That dissolves all our anger and pain.
We are cured by compassion, healed through Mans' empathy;
Love frees the slave of his chains.

Perfect cohesion and freedom are found
In each atom, each flower, each tree;
In rivers that flow into crystal blue oceans
As well as in you and in me.

Arrogant thinking or pride leads to falls,
Once I'm upright again it's a fact
That I am not punished by past flaws but rather
Life will mirror, to perfection, how I react.

Perfection is Love, there are Laws on this Earth
Which hold true for the sea and the sky
And the bonding of Love with our Human existence
Tells God we are ready to fly.

About the Poet

Greg Wright was born in 1949, a late bloomer baby-boomer. From an early age people said that someone should follow Greg around and write down his insightful and witty observations. Being there were no takers he assumed this "yoke of honor" himself.

Readers have described him as a cross between Dr. Seuss and Sigmund Freud. Therefore, he describes himself as a Seussenfreudian Poet. Since April 4th, 1999 he has dedicated his writings to Peace, humor and contemplative poetry. A big fan of both Rudyard Kipling and his hero, his father, he currently is alive and kicking in Wilmington, Delaware.

Made in the USA
Middletown, DE
29 March 2024

52039214R00051